Bookends

Beth Robb

BookLeaf Publishing
India | USA | UK

Presentation by *BookLeaf Publishing*

Web: www.bookleafpub.com

E-mail: info@bookleafpub.com

ISBN: 9789360943929

First edition 2024

To the greatest loves of my life. LWR and EFR, I was incomplete before you, and so incredibly proud you're mine

Love,

Mom

ACKNOWLEDGEMENT

Teachers have been a great inspiration to me all of my life, and there are a couple whose guidance I have carried with me in all things. The late Christine Parker taught me in second grade to be honest, to work hard, and not be afraid to use your imagination. Donna Griffin, my high school English teacher, was a stickler for the rules of language (I'm sorry Mrs. Griffin, I know I've broken a lot of your rules!), and I hear her voice when I write even an email or patient visit note. But my favorite teachers were in my home. My parents have taught me life lessons no classroom ever could. Lessons of being kind, giving your time to others, working hard and what real love looks like. I hope I have made all of these people proud.

PREFACE

I've always wanted to write a book. The problem has been that I have so many ideas and have read so many books, that I always believed I could never complete anything that someone would even want to read. As I've gotten older, I've developed a bucket list which keeps growing by the day. Writing book is on that list. I love a challenge, so this was the best way to break through my fears and just get it done. Poems feel personal. While some of the works included are just imaginings, some are straight out of this crazy life of mine. It feels raw and scary to be putting it out there on display. Kinda like those dreams where you get on the school bus naked. Hopefully, like in those dreams, no one will be able to notice my anxiety and will just be able to enjoy them. But if you do notice, I hope you will read anyway and find courage yourself to take on something on your bucket list. Let me tell you, finishing this big check mark feels good!

Like Riding a Bike

Mom: Day One
Scared but ready,
Strong yet unsteady.
No manual, no brakes.
No practice, no mistakes.

Mom: Day 1825
Trainers on, Peddle fast
Run beside, make it last.

Mom: Day 6570
Trainers off, on their own.
Just 2 wheels, the time has flown.
Run behind a second, but soon you know
Go on ahead,
that's it,
Let go.

Listen for Our Forever

Searching for the answer.
When did it change?
When did TOGETHER
Become ME and YOU not us?

The light that shone each time you came home,
Now blinks, and is quickly shuttered.

LISTEN for the sound that calls you back to me.
The sound of MY heart,
When mixed with yours,
Is the sound of our love,
Our life,
Our forever.

Brain Drain

I'm going to try to explain
The jumble of thoughts within my brain.
I used to be a procrastinator.
Why do now what I can put off for later?
As I grow older, things get worse.
Forget the bills, and lose my purse.
Last minute panics when things aren't complete.
Always enough ketchup, yet nothing to eat.
I know I'm not stupid, I need to do better.
But hard as I try, I can't get it together.
Dishes stack up, clothes lay in piles.
Hiding my "crazy" behind closed doors and
smiles.
I grow weary as there's chaos around.
Maybe a doctor can make my mind sound.
Get it together get past this messy sorrow.
I am ready to make the appointment.
I'll call....tomorrow.

Get Up, Get Out, Get Away

Her plan was always to
Grow up.
Get out.
Get Away.
Big Plans, Big Dreams.
To create a space to become herself, by herself.
Eyes Wide Open.
Be brave, No Fear.
New world of bricks and books and higher
education.
New faces, New Places.
A time to learn and a time to take chances.
Trusting that the goodness she's always known
in everyone.
After dark, After hours, After just one drink.
Out of her element, out of patience.
Says he'll drive you home, says don't walk alone.
Hesitant but she reluctantly agrees.
Pushed In, Held Down.
Wait. Stop. No.
Time to fight, Time to Run.
Get Up.
Get Out.
Get Away.

Big Failure, Big Mistake. Doubting everything
she learned and knew about herself.
Eyes swollen, afraid of everything.
Don't talk about it. Don't think about it.
Need to go back. Need the old places, need
familiar faces.
Let them believe it's just too far, just too hard,
and she'll never
Grow Up
Get Out or
Get Away.

Betty June's Beauty Salon

A little trailer
Pepsi bottles stacked by the door.
Beyond the entrance was so much more.
Clouds of Aqua Net and high teased hair.
Combs and brushes and pins to spare.
A wash, a set, a permanent wave.
The best part was all the advice that you gave.
Don't forget to vote,it's your privilege and right.
Always help others, always kiss goodnight.
Stay in school and study hard.
Roll the dice, don't show your cards.
Laugh at yourself, keep an eye on your brother.
Don't go to bed mad, forgive your mother.
Drive past, honk the horn, you'd pop out your
head.
I am so proud of the life that you lead.
"See you tomorrow. I love you. Don't tell 'em
you're Grandma's best friend."
Never dreaming our time in the "shop" would
end.
Who knew your heart would take you from me,
And your shampoo bowl, my favorite place to
be?

Chinese Fire Drill

Green Light!
I've got shotgun, you've got the wheel.
Jo and Kitty pile in the back.
Red Light!
Throw it in park, throw open the doors.
Run in circles. Screaming and laughing.
Green Light!
You've got shotgun, I've got the wheel.
Kitty and Jo pile in the back. Throw it in drive,
and a few blocks later,
Red light!
Throw open the doors! Run in circles, lose a
shoe. Run into each other.
Green Light!
Kitty's got shotgun, Jo has the wheel.
You piled in the back.
I watch the taillights fading and hope someone
catches
What went wrong with our Chinese Fire Drill.

Who, What, Where, When, How?

Where do I go?
What do I do?
Who can I trust, when I can't trust you?
How do I move?
How do I wake?
How do I sleep, when the dreams I can't take?
When did it start?
When will it end?
How can I know it won't happen again?
I choose to go forward.
I choose to move on.
I choose you.
I hope I'm not wrong.

Your Hand and Mine

YOUR HANDS
Pink, tiny and fragile in
MY HANDS
The day you were born. It's hard to let go of
YOUR HANDS
exploring and learning while holding
MY HANDS
Hugging you, guiding you, then letting go when
YOUR HANDS
Hold tiny hands of your own, then
MY HANDS
Are praying for the places you go, until
YOUR HANDS
Big and strong and warm, hold
MY HANDS
That are now frail and worn. And I know that
one last time, I must let go.

A Life in the Day

The sun rises on a new day.
Full of promise and things to come.
A cloudless sky, the heat of the sun,
And a breeze that makes you smile as you turn
your face up to catch the light.
The hours pass quickly on this bright morn.

Midday brings a change to the light.
Shadows stretch across the landscape and dark
clouds roll in.

Winds pick up, thunder claps and lightening
streaks across the once peaceful sky.

Rain pelts your turned up face and you wonder
why this chaos has disrupted what had once
been such an idyllic day.

The hours in the eye of the storm stretch
endlessly and it's hard to believe that,
As evening approaches, those dark clouds will
lessen in the sky.

Shadows shorten. The sweet, clean smell after
the rain provides a pause before you turn to face
the twilight's brief hours.

Cooler breezes, purpling sunset.
Quiet, slower hours as the sun fades in the
distance to a fast approaching night.

As you reflect there in that moment, you come
to understand that if it weren't for the heat of the
morning, the storms of the afternoon, and the
tranquility of twilight, you could never have
arrived to this place.

This hour.

This most all encompassing, star filled night.

Wanderlust

The dots on a map they beckon me
to fly where the four winds lead.
I long to go to exotic lands
From all the books I read.

To Go and see the Isles of Greece,
To Spend a week in France.
To Roll the dice on the Vegas strip.
Give Switzerland another chance.

I want to explore all fifty states,
and I long for sunny beaches
A mountain peak, a sunset cruise
The taste of Georgia peaches.

Wanderlust, it dares me go
to Mexico and Rome,
But whenever my life leads me away,
My heart always calls me home.

Days Gone By

A telephone hangs on the kitchen wall,
A cell is only in jail.
Notes are left when you're leaving home.
There is no such thing as email.
A text is a book, a tweet is a bird.
A map is to get where you're going,
The only net is Aquanet,
And to "like" is not an act, its a feeling.
Libraries are for research,
and for keeping info straight,
Google is what your eyes can do,
and a post holds up a gate.
A laptop is my granny's quilt,
Amazon a giant river.
Tick tock goes the hallway clock
Only pizza gets delivered.
Comparing today with eighties ways, I miss the
days gone by.
But the fact that now a filter can make me
skinny, not coffee,
Brings a tear of joy to my eye!

To the Little Girl I Used to Be

To that little girl I used to be,

You are enough.
Don't measure your worth with someone else's
ruler.
The you in your mind that is not afraid.
The you that reaches further, dreams bigger,
beyond the limits you have set in place for
yourself. Protect her.

You are brave. Be brave beyond your borders.
The borders of your familiar, safe space.
Beyond what is comfortable, because
Comfortable is not growing. Step into the light
you hold inside you.

You are resilient. When adversity threatens to
dull your shine, don't let the darkness win.
Not every path you choose will be paved and
straight.
Sometimes the potholes, curves and dirt packed
roads will lead to the most beautiful of
destinations.

You, my girl, are beautiful.
Look at the reflection of your smile on the faces
of others.
Mirrors lie.
Hearts do not.

You will be amazing.
Hold your head high and
turn down the sounds of self doubt.
Wear glitter.
Wear makeup.
Wear whatever makes you feel good. There are
no rules or molds.

And most of all, I will be waiting. I will take it
from here.

The locket

A round gold locket with filigree
handed down from my grandma to me.
Two tiny photos loose in the clasp.
Is how they sealed their promise to last.

It wasn't easy and ended too soon,
A life full of joy and with trials.
They both are gone, but love carries on,
and the locket still hold in their smiles.

Only one was here when I graduated
Neither on my wedding day.
That locked to kept them near my heart,
and my daughter wears it today.

Opportunities of Dying?

If I told you a person who is dying has
opportunities, would you scoff?
Would you say that dying is the end and there
are no opportunities left?
I would say they have opportunities.
Opportunities To say the things they have been
holding in their heart without fear.
To say I love you without risk of being
misunderstood.
To say I am sorry to someone they think they
have wronged.
To say thank you to the spouse who has been
beside them through struggles of marriage,
children and illness.
To say Good-bye.
See you soon if their beliefs so align.
To close their eyes one last time knowing
they've said what they needed to say.
But I would also say why wait?
Why risk not taking these opportunities sooner?
Saying daily I love you's, I'm sorry's and thank
you's.
Celebrating, rejoicing and renewing
relationships, Every day you are afforded.

Knowing you are dying shouldn't be the trigger
to live a loving, forgiving, grateful life.
And you will close your eyes every day knowing
you've said what you needed to say.

Man of my Dreams

I see you in my dreams.
I think of the warm day we met so long ago
I wonder where you have gone and if I will ever
see you again.

Your memory elicits an easier time
When I didn't need to impress you
And you would come to me without me having
to call your name.

I hear our song,
playing on the winds of summers past.
As I sit on the porch this early evening
it echos through my mind as if it were yesterday.

I look to the street where we first met and
I cannot believe my eyes.
Good Humor man you've returned to me at last.

For Emilee

If you only knew
The prayers my heart has prayed for you.
The hours I have lain awake
Worrying about the path you'll take.
Did you feel my love when I wasn't there?
Do you know the strength of your Mother's
prayer?
If you only knew
How proud I am each day, of you.
Your strength to stand for what is right.
Your grace to always Be the light
that worldly darkness tries to hide
Do you feel the depth of your Mother's Pride?
I hope you feel your Mother's Prayers,
I hope you know I'm Proud of You.
I hope you know the love of a daughter
Who will be the joy that I known in you.

For Lucas

My sweet boy
So much I have wished for you.
A gentle heart that loves beyond the reaches of
each new horizon.
A peaceful mind that allows you to dream
outside all possibilities.
A bold spirit to guide you on the path of
adventure and goodness and
Strong arms to work hard to achieve your goals.

And then I realized that you,
my son, embody all of these things,
and in you, my wishes have come true.

Our Moon girl

This little pup came into our lives
as a ball of fur and fluff
the face of a husky, the size of a toy,
she wants you to think she is tough.
She takes lots of naps, she hates the sweeper,
Gets the zoomies and barks at my shoe.
She sleeps on my head, she sleeps in my bed,
one eye is brown and one is blue.
She's our Luna, our Lu, our Chooch, she has so
many
names.
I just know since she moved in,
our house is not the same.

Home

My parent's house is always open,
Nan's teapot's always on.
Friends are always welcome.
Pop's always mowing the lawn.

The pool is always sparkling,
the pantry always full.
Its where you learned that God is Good
and to follow the Golden Rule.

There's always a spare toothbrush,
plenty of hugs to spare.
I sleep easier every night just knowing that
they're there.

Life has spread us out a bit,
our family has grown.
We all have houses of our own,
but that house will always be HOME

When I Grow Up

There are so many things that I want to be when
I grow up.
I am still struggling to decide what I will choose.
The harried wife who never quite gets the
housework done.
The busy mom who taxis the kids around.
The crazy neighbor who wears sweaters on her
dog.
The woman who serves on committees and asks
for funds.
The nurse who cares for people in the
community.
The friend who will drop everything if you need
me.
The daughter who appreciates every second of
family time.
The traveler who wants to see and explore the
world.
This list goes on and on, but I know what I don't
have to ever consider being when I grown up.
Bored

All Good Things must End

You've heard it said "All good things must end".
A good movie,
A good book.
A good meal.
These things surely do have an ending.
The difference between one good ending and
another however, is the feeling that you are left
with.
A good movie or book may leave you on the
edge of your seat, anticipating a sequel, or
crying because the ending left you feeling
emotional and wanting more.
A good meal may end but the feeling of fullness
stays with you and gets you through until the
next time you break your fast.
All good lives, too, must come to an end. What
matters then are the feelings left behind and
those experiencing them.
In dying, are you on the edge of your seat,
anticipating the sequel of an afterlife promised
by God?
Are you feeling saddened by the loss of a good
life of a loved one and left wanting more to the
story that was unwritten?

Are you full from the love that has been left behind and will carry on for the next generation or until you meet around Heaven's table once again?
If you are looking for a good ending, write it yourself.

www.ingramcontent.com/pod-product-compliance
Lightning Source LLC
LaVergne TN
LVHW021329200726
843509LV00014B/2456